The Sky is

NOT

the Limit!

A Book Of
Empowering Poetry

Alicea Davis

Esteem Builders Publications Co.
Pontiac, Michigan, USA

Anica + Emery
With God,
there are no
limits

Aileen Davis
3-23-19

BUILDERS
PUBLICATIONS CO.

*"Publishing books that heal, empower, and build up the minds of others
for the betterment of society."*

The Sky is NOT the Limit! A Book of Empowering Poetry
Copyright © 2008, 2016 Alicea Davis - 2nd Edition

A Note from the Publisher:
Mrs. Davis began exploring her artistic journey under the pseudonym "MEe," which communicated her awareness of her place in the universe. Later, after shedding the shadows of darkness and fear, she shared her visions of the world and reclaimed her birthright as Alicea Crafter. Hence, astute observers will note that the art contained on the pages of this book are signed "A Crafter." Today, she joyfully continues to share her artistic gift with the world as she carries the surname of beloved husband, Benjamin. These paintings mark her journey of self-discovery and are joyfully used in this book with permission.

Esteem Builders Publications Co.
P.O. Box 431151
Pontiac, MI 48343 USA

URL: http://www.esteembuilderspublications.com

ISBN 13:   978-0-9979671-1-1

Cover and interior paintings by Alicea Davis

Edited by Esteem Builders Publications Co.

Cover and interior design by Christina Dixon

Printed in the United States of America

*This book is devoted
to your spiritual empowerment.*

Table of Contents

Part Two: Enlightened Love

Part Three: Barriers Broken

* Indicates poems added since the first edition of this book.

Part One:
Infinite
Possibilities

Infinite Possibilities by Alicea Davis

This painting symbolizes the unlimited potential that we can discover within ourselves.

Desire

We follow this drive
that lets us know we are alive.
Making us want to do more than just simply survive,
fueling our motivation to thrive.

It is this inner desire
that inspires us to go higher,
though going further may not extinguish this fire.

Because we can always go on just a little bit more.
There will always be another unopened door.

And knowing that life's process
may never come to an end,
will cause some to stand still and others to begin again.

Dream Again

People what are you settling for?
Do you think you can acquire just a little bit more?
Some might be looking funny,
thinking that I'm just talking about money.
But this is about seeking knowledge,
and about someone starting or finishing college.

It's about that goal you have in your heart.
It may even be a business
that you've been wanting to start.
Is it false or is it true?
Do these things apply to you?

Now I know that some may be comfortable and content,
with just getting by paying the rent.
I know that some people just sit and pray,
simply standing by, waiting on judgment day.
Just thought I should tell you that it's okay,
to make your trip on earth a more comfortable stay.

Sometime ago it was accepted;
this lifestyle that was selected.
But as a child, what did you desire to be?
What was your vision? What did you see?
When was the day that you forfeited your fight?
You were free to dream, but you gave up that right.

It doesn't matter what is the color of your skin,
or the neighborhood that you grew up in.
Your parents may have not been around.
Your family and friends may have put you down.
But you have the right to dream at night.
You have a future that is fruitful and bright!

Do you think that there's inside information,
flowing outside of your community,
and that the knowledge is controlled
while there is no sense of unity?
Well, even if there is truth in that,
you still must consider this simple fact.

There is a brain inside of your head,
with ideas for you to get ahead.
There is a heart inside of your chest,
full of passion for you to be your best.
And there is a voice inside of your mouth,
with positive words that have to come out.

And just as sure as you can blink,
you have that right to dream and think.
No one on earth can give you the permission
to accept and complete your chosen mission.
The mission to fulfill your calling in life.
The mission to finally get this thing right.

God has some major plans for you.
Just put Him first in all you do.
But do something!

Contribute! Participate!
Inside of you is a person that is great.
You can't lose hope! You can't lose sight!
You are free to dream, and you must exercise that right.
Focus on the vision that you have within.
Start living your life and dream again.

Begin

How will we finish if we never start?
Will we know when things are together,
if they have never fallen apart?
We will not reach our destination,
nor our reward at the end,
if we do not have in our hearts the courage to begin.

That's why I have decided that I will soar.
And that I will cherish my life even more.
After the ups and downs, I've done the math.
I'm factoring in a different path.

Although I cannot see my future, the Light will lead me.
My courage and faith
will nourish and feed me.
And before I can walk through that brand new door,
I must appreciate where I was before.

As I observe my history, I see a story.
It was investing in pain that earned my glory.
Victory has always been mine. I even gain when I lose.
So no matter my weakness, going forward I will choose.

These journeys will last me my whole life long.
I'm headed right to where I belong.
Although I am not sure what is in store at the end,
one thing is for certain, I will begin.

At Night

When it is hard for me to see the light,
my favorite time of day is night.
Because when the sun is brightly shining,
I hide my tears and mute my whining.

But at night it is hard for others to see,
the pain and hurt inside of me.
For my body is not as tired as my soul.
And I wonder, "How I will accomplish my goal?"

At night it's safe to express my fear and doubt,
by lying down in my bed without standing out.
I imagine that I've had a dynamic day,
although so many obstacles are still in my way.

While I wonder if I have done my best,
the moon gives me permission to rest.
Soon I will reach that special place.
But first I have some fears to face.

Fears that are inside of me.
Fears that are not always easy to see.
I know that this phase is only a test,
and I must complete my chosen quest.

Facing trial and error in the broad day light.
Then expressing my fears as I lay at night.

Waking Up

Lord,
thank You for waking me up this morning
and starting me on my way.
Thank You for showing me more of you each day.

Thank You for managing this beautiful earth,
where every day is a gift, just as the day of my birth.

For every second that You bless me to see,
tells me that You have more plans for me.

Are You Sure?

Are You sure, Lord?
Are You sure about me?
Am I supposed to take literally
the visions that I see?

Is my mind supposed to believe,
the things that I am chosen to receive?
I mean no disrespect.
I just want to double check.

I just want to double check that You are sure.
Can make my heart and mind pure?
For so long I have been ashamed.
I thought that my struggles were a game,
and that I was the one to blame.

But You allowed my hard times to happen
for my greater good,
while my instabilities were misunderstood.
But now that I am stable,
I know that You are able,
and that the vision I saw was not a fable.

What I saw was so great
I thought that You made a cosmic mistake,
and that this place was not chosen for me,
because I could not handle the thought of victory.

Are You Sure? cont'd

For a long time, I have been down,
with a lot of negative people around.
And I started to think so lowly of myself
that I couldn't fathom a life of wealth and good health.
And even though this world may be full of coldness,
with Your help I can face it with boldness,
and work my assignment with the strength to endure,
because You have chosen me for this,
and You are absolutely sure.

This poem is dedicated to my brother Michael.

How Tall

How tall do I have to be
before I'm recognized as a tree?
Am I a plant when I am just a seed,
if it's only time that I need?

How long must I wait,
before the world will see me as great?
I know that today I look very small,
but in my heart I am tall.

It took some time but now I know,
I also need sunlight and rain to grow.
I have to do more than just simply wait.
I must be buried alive before I germinate.

This growth process that was designed for me,
will make me more than just a possibility.
So underneath the ground I will be,
until I begin to emerge as a tree.

I have to absorb the air all around,
as I rise out of the ground.
Oxygen is what I need to live.
It is also what I need to give.

Now I know that becoming a tree,
isn't a reward just for me.
But when I am rooted in my chosen space.
I will make this world a better place.

Although I am just a seed today,
I've gotten to the point where I can say,
that I will be a great and mighty tree,
no matter how tall I get to be.

My Dreams

My dreams are real,
and my heart can feel,
that time will reveal,
what the world can't steal.

Gifts

Our gifts are meant to edify one another,
and to unify each other as sister and brother.
We must understand
the higher purpose and plan.

Together we can conquer the darkest beast,
once our gifts and inner powers are released.
The chaos will cease,
as we work towards peace.

We all have contributions to give,
and a better life to live.
So please find what your purpose in life is about,
so that the rest of the world won't be left out.

Fear of Life

When I saw a vision of my future history,
I felt robbed of my life's biggest mystery.
As I discovered my chosen destiny,
the darkest cloud swept over me.

I felt like my achievements would bring me to my death.
So holding out on my talent would allow me to
keep my breath.
I doubted that I was worthy of a path so great.
How could someone like me participate?
I was poisoned with self-hate.

I thought that I would only play an insignificant part.
So the burden of life weighed heavy in my heart.
I questioned if my visions were real and
if my dreams would last.
I was afraid of my future, and I had outgrown my past.

It felt like present time was a trap.
Because I was shown my destination but not given a map.
I was frustrated with the purpose behind this
and I questioned why do we even exist?

Searching for the meaning of life
actually hindered me from living
because I was ungrateful for what The Creator was giving.
I was given a task so divine
with rewards that were exclusively mine.

But the fear of my path had me paralyzed,
until the moment I realized,
that no matter what my mind wanted to believe,
I have a job to do so I cannot leave.

Then I accepted that my fate was great
and that my future could no longer wait.
I embraced the many gifts that I have to give.
Facing the fear of life with the desire to live.

Fears Faced

I used to keep my dreams locked up inside.
My goals were something I would try to hide.
Success was a scenario that I tried to avoid,
because I was so paranoid.

It didn't matter if my dreams were small or great.
I would get so nervous, that I would just wait.
I wanted to move, but I would hesitate.
As if I were delaying some terrible fate.

Then one day
I heard God say,
"Alicea, what's wrong with you?
Don't you realize that you have work to do?"

I said, "I know Lord, I really want to,
but what if all of my fears come true?"
He said, "Take this journey. Your path has been laid.
Why are you waiting? Why are you afraid?"

I said, "If I take this road, my life will change.
My relationships with people might get strange.
I don't want my happiness to make others feel bad.
I might want the ordinary life I already had.
If I change my life, I might feel regret,
and I don't want to be viewed as a major threat."

Then God said back to me,
"My child, when will you begin to see?
How much more obvious can it be?
What will it take to prove,
that you're already a target?
This is why you have to move!
There's no need to worry because I've got your back.
I've already blocked the enemy's attack.
And it's not about what people may want you to be.
If you don't shine your light, you'll have to answer to me!"

With that being said,
I started moving ahead.
My fears became something that I no longer fed.
And those same talents that I used to hide,
are now being multiplied.

Now, I am here to tell you that your calling is great.
And that fear and hate is the enemy's bait.
He wants to steal your dreams before it's too late.
He wants to distract you before you open your eyes.
He wants to tear you down before you realize
that God has invested unique talents in you.
And they are connected to what you've been chosen to do.

Your gifts are not for your pride or vanity.
They are contributions to humanity.
Fulfilling your purpose in life is a deal that is sweet.
Because pursuing your passions will feel like a treat.

Fears Faced cont'd

I know it may sound too good to be true.
But it has happened for me, and it can happen for you.
Just silence the thoughts in your mind that are depressing
and dark.
And don't leave this earth without making your mark.

A mark that can never be erased
as long as your fears are faced.

A Secret to Success

There is something that you owe yourself,
if you want good health and a life full of wealth.
God has some major plans for you,
but first you have some inner work to do.

Because there is a reason why your dreams don't last.
It's because you've been holding on to your past.
It eats away at your success,
this anger and pain that was repressed.

I know how that person put trauma on you,
and acted as if there's only drama on you.
But only you are carrying this heavy load,
while they barely even remember that episode.

They may have tested you or rejected you,
and you want to hold on to a grudge, like the rest would do.
But you must let go.
Because you will not be able to grow.

There may be so many years wasted before you realize,
that you were spiritually paralyzed.
All those projects you started that never got finished,
was because a piece of your soul was diminished.
But when you let go, you will be replenished.

You must release the pain that you went through,
and break those chains that are binding you.

A Secret to Success cont'd

This same release has happened to me,
and it feels so good to live so free!

Your true purpose in life will come and find you,
once you have the courage to leave your past behind you.
It doesn't matter if the tears
have been flowing for many years.

Even strangers can identify who you are,
because of how soon you show them your scar.
You are in denial because you think you are fine,
when in reality you are living in past time.

Your pain can be conquered with the power of love,
because you have help from up above.
Whether you were shot, abused or even molested,
what's done is done. Now only you can accept it.

It may be hard to believe, but after a while,
they may decide to reconcile.
But if they are still rejecting, you can't stop.
Because jaws will drop once you make it to the top.

But first it has to be in your heart to forgive.
Then a prosperous life you are sure to live.
And this fortune that I am talking about,
you will possess both inside and out.
And your bright future will prove the rest,
once you apply to your life this secret to success.
Forgive.

Forgiveness Is

In order to live,
we must forgive.
Forgiving is seeing the purpose
Underneath the surface.

Knowing that what seems scary
is oftentimes necessary.
Although the pain hurts and your heart may cry,
you must search for that reason why.

Figure out why that challenge was chosen for you.
Follow the Light to your breakthrough.
Let it be clearly understood
that the struggle was designed for your greater good.

Then take your soul through the much needed repairs,
freeing yourself from heavy burdens and cares.
For when a trial has successfully made you stronger,
you do not have to endure that pain much longer.

Though you may move on to greater tests,
you will achieve your spiritual best.
Remembering that the lightest way to live,
is to respect your test and thankfully forgive.

Being Successful

Sometimes being successful
is just simply living
by loving, caring, sharing and giving.

Sometimes being successful
is just being content,
knowing that your life was heaven sent.

Sometimes being successful
is working your God given plan
even if it is not approved by man.

Sometimes being successful
is ignoring the concept of success.
because to be alive is to truly be blessed.

Moving On

At times when I am afraid and all alone,
I want to go back to my comfort zone.
That's when I need more courage to search and roam,
because I still have not found my home.

I desire to reach a time and place,
where I can thrive in my chosen space.
But when my past and future play tug-of-war,
I tend to lose track of what I am searching for.

That's when I wonder if there will always be,
a sense of uncertainty inside of me.
I ask, "Could this be the purpose of trust,
to not know my outcome yet go on I must?"

I have to keep moving. I cannot stay in this spot,
because this life of mine is all that I've got.
I know where I've been, and I want to see more.
So I'll just have to walk toward that unopened door.

My Epiphany

It got to the point where I couldn't help but see,
that there was something wrong with me.
Before now, I was in so much denial
that I would put everyone else on trial.

I'd say, "He has a problem and so does she.
and the whole world is taking things out on me!"
I would live my life day after day
disregarding what others would try and say
about me and my problem.

To me, the ones who tried to give me a hand,
were only more people who did not understand.
I didn't know that their criticism
was out of care and concern.
So when they stretched out to reach me,
they would just get burned.

Burned by the fire that was consuming me.
Burned by my problem that I couldn't see.
I was full of so much stress and strife,
they would cut me off just to save their own life.

But I didn't get it because I didn't know.
So, I let a lot of valuable people go.
When they would walk away, I would just say, "Bye!"
Not knowing that my problem was the reason why.

And as my problem grew taller,
my circles were much smaller.
Until it just got to the point where I couldn't help but see,
that there was something wrong with me.

And it was really a close call,
Because I began to think that I didn't need people at all.
Until I reached a place on my journey to success
where I'd have to turn back or face my mess.

Face my problem that others were talking about,
my problem that I could no longer doubt.
A problem that when I finally saw it,
I was in so much awe of it.

It was hideous, and it was huge. It had such a magnitude,
I just knew it was affecting my attitude.
It was painful to see it.
And it hurt even more for me to be it.

Immediately I said,
"It's no wonder why the people don't call!
It's no wonder why I started to fall."
I went from mad to sad, from sad to glad.
I started thinking about the relationships that I had.

I thought about all of the people that walked away,
and how their absence contributed to my epiphany today.
And if I saw them again, all I would say is,
"Thank you for showing me that people deserve more.
And I don't blame you for walking out of that door."

My Epiphany cont'd

And for the few people that didn't give up.
Although it was rough, you've had more than enough.
Your love saved my life, you saved the day.
You inspired me to improve my way.

And as my hopes and dreams come true,
it would be an honor to share them with you.
Still I am faced with the reality
that identifying my problem is just a part of the strategy.

But half of my battle is already won,
and I know that I will overcome.
Because it got to the point
where I couldn't help but see,
that there was something wrong with me.
And that is my epiphany.

Will the People

I know that I am different,
but some may think that I am the same.
So I am not sure what the people will hear
when they say my name.

Will the people who've betrayed me
think that I am still upset?
Will the ones who've I've unintentionally hurt
believe that I have sincere regrets?

As I perform my chosen task,
people from my past
may think that I am wearing a mask.
But they will know that I've changed,
if they would only ask.

So I tell myself that God can use,
whatever undeserving soul that He may choose.
And since He was merciful enough to choose me,
I'll just have to be the best me that I can be.

Because I want to swim, but I may sink,
if I worry about what the people will think.

Eye of My Storm

My storm is not over. I'm only standing in the eye.
I have to brace myself before the rest passes by.
I cannot come out of the shelter. I must stay inside.
Although the sun is still shining, I still have to hide.

Because my storm is not over, It's only taking a break.
And it's too early to know how much damage it will make.
It will seem like two storms although I know it's only one.
And I'll have to remember that, when the rest of it comes.

In life it seems like certain problems are new.
When the old ones are still just passing through.
I feel the beating rain, and I hear the fierce wind.
Yet I know that my storm will eventually end.

Calming Down

I used to be busy, but I was not productive.
I wanted to build, but I was not constructive.
I would see my target but would miss my aim.
Then I realized that my burdens were the blame.

The day that piece of straw broke the camel's back
the day I had a severe anxiety attack,
the day that forced me to get my mind on track.
So I agreed to live in a psych ward for a week,
to relax and listen to the experts speak.

They assessed my situation and this was the bottom line,
They said, "You're a talented girl, and you'll be just fine.
Just live your life one day at a time."

But that was the biggest challenge for me.
After realizing the potential of what I could be,
my future was all that my heart could see,
but not worrying about tomorrow has set me free.

My mental slate became organized and clean.
My calming down and starting over felt like a dream.
It was as if I had a second chance at life.
And God reduced my stress and eliminated my strife.

Although I trust and hope that my future is swell,
I can let go of the stress because only time will tell.

Conscience

I have no choice
but to listen to my inner voice.
This whisper inside of me can not be ignored.
It is something to be adored.

When there is no trusted advisor around,
there is inner guidance to be found.
As I focus closely, I find
That many solutions are in the quiet thoughts of my mind.

I used to experience self-doubt a bit,
And I would talk myself right out of it.
Then later on I would regretfully say,
"I should've went with the answer that came my way."

Following my inner compass keeps me on the road,
without carrying such a heavy load.
Listening to this voice has set me free,
and it will not be taken away from me.

Inner Space

The universe is an amazing place to explore,
and in your mind is so much more.
But when you fear the journey that's inside of your head,
you'll only search the outer space instead.

Since I Became Conscious

There was a time in my life when I could only see
the things that would just revolve around me.
I'd think, "How complicated can this world be?"
Until one day the truth came and set me free.
The day that I became *conscious*.

And ever since my mind has been enlightened,
my vital signs and senses
have also become heightened.
Now when I watch TV,
subliminal messages are obvious to me.

I hear concealed phrases that aren't blatantly said.
And I see how the masses are influenced and led.
I feel a new found passion inside of my heart,
with a deeper love for people that sets me apart.

I can smell hatred and corruption from a mile away.
The odor reeks in the environment day after day.
Thankfully the taste of love is so divine
that I was instantly addicted. It must always be mine.

Since I became conscious, my priorities have rearranged.
Even my taste in men has changed.
At first he had to earn a certain number of dollars.
He had to associate with the wealthy
and rich white collars.
His car had to be brand spanking new,
and he had to be impressed with my fake hairdo.
But those were the days when I didn't have a clue.

And now that my heart and mind are more free
I can really get what is in store for me.
I'm appreciating various manifestations of wealth.
And above all, is the value of knowing God
and myself.

Since I became conscious,
some people think that I'm **out there**.
They are absolutely right! That's why I don't care.
And I don't plan on going anywhere.
I'm not moving backwards. I'm only moving ahead.
I'm purifying myself from the destruction I was fed.
It was hard to admit that I was being misled.

Many are called to this truth, but few are selected.
I think it's because so many people reject it.
You must be ready in case this truth is brought to you.
If you're not open, then it cannot be taught to you.

If this truth is something that you are blessed to see,
then hear this poem again to see how different it will be.
So you can gain a better understanding of me
and why I've changed
since I became
conscious.

Judgment

If we are free to live however we may...
If we are directly affected by what we do and say...
If rewards or retributions can come our way...
Is everyday a judgment day?

Temple

My body is a temple,
and it is just that simple.
It houses God's Holy Spirit that dwells there.
So I have to administer to it special care.

It is my physical shell.
It's how I see, hear, feel, taste, and smell.
The more that my body is nourished,
the more that I am free to flourish.

On earth I have a lot of work to do,
and my body must last until I'm through.
Before, I did not initiate my care-giving role,
because I thought it was totally out of my control.

I used to view life in reverse,
thinking that my body would break down first.
But I realize that, for now, I need it.
So I am careful with how I treat and feed it.

It could be more complicated,
but for me it's simple.
There is light inside of my God-given temple.

God

Through the gospel of Jesus,
God has been my guide.
His presence was all around me,
but I had to let Him inside.

Why Choose Jesus?

My mind was tossing to and fro,
when I was searching for a new spiritual truth to know.
You see, an unhealthy Christian church is where I was
born and raised.
So later, I went through a tumultuous questioning phase.
Questions that would keep me up at night,
when something in my mind just didn't feel right.

I had outgrown religion. I needed something more.
A true relationship with God was what I was yearning for.
I slowly left the faith of my youth,
to seek secular enlightenment and truth.

Then my mind opened up like a treasure map.
But each path that I took was a part of Satan's trap.
Subconsciously, I was really on the path to find me.
Deep inside, I desired to see how powerful I could be.

Satan tempted me with the pride of life. I thought I was tall.
but the deceiver knew that pride would lead to my fall.
Yet the fall helped me realize that every incomplete truth
is a lie.
So I reconciled my faith in Christ, and some still want to
know why.

Why choose Jesus?
Because He frees us.
I am free from the penalty of sin, and the victory is won.
A new covenant with God has already begun.

No matter what many try to say,
only one road leads to God, and Jesus is the way.
This earth is temporary. I could die tonight.
So I want to be set for eternal life.

Why Choose Jesus? cont'd

Jesus is the Son of God. This I believe.
He died for my sins, and His forgiveness is what I am
blessed to receive.

Some may say, "Christianity, Alicea? I thought you were
enlightened."
I inform them that my mind is not oppressed or frightened.
But what I needed was for my soul to be heightened.
My heart loves true love,
Because I am a child of my God above.

Before the Creator said, "Let there be light,"
He knew that it I would become a follower of Christ.
I know it's hard to look past the faults of man.
This also led me astray, so I understand.
I know many horrible things have been done
in the name of Christianity.
But those were misrepresentations of the truth, you see.
That's why I pray that the Church will show
the true beauty of the cross,
so that searching souls everywhere will no longer be lost.

No matter what language we use to speak Jesus' name,
our faith will be rewarded just the same.
At the name of Jesus, every knee will bow.
But you can choose life and surrender now.

Because every soul on earth will exist
in heaven or hell for eternity.
An eternal life or an eternal death?
Which one will you see?
But take it from me,

Christianity is not religious bondage
for a soul tormenting in fear.
But a loving relationship with God
because He wants you near.

Even if I live over 100 years,
I want to do it victoriously and live through my tears.
I choose Jesus because His truth has made me free.
He has the greatest love for you and me.

I choose Jesus so I can live life on earth more abundantly,
I'm not just proclaiming the truth to you redundantly.
I could go on and on about the rewards
of God's spiritual wealth.
But Jesus is a choice that you have to
choose for yourself.

Discovery

I started to search through my mind,
because I wanted to see what I would find.
Knowing that my intellect was healthy and strong
I ventured inside to see where I belong.

And today I am at peace because I have found it.
A place where I'll rest, now that I am grounded.
I am no longer a pilgrim exploring my own inner land,
but now a citizen in a world that I am starting to
understand.

Although I've found this place I am not through,
for I have some building and growing to do.
That's why I cherish this ground where I am now planted.
My inner territory must not be taken for granted.

I crossed my personal deserts and seas,
just to find a place to be at ease.
The exclusive journey is not just for me,
but also for all humanity.

A world of peace can be found from anywhere.
Just search inside, and you'll be there.
I knew who the world wanted me to be,
but I customized my life to represent me.

I look forward to a life of prosperity and wealth,
because I have found God, and I am learning myself.

Like Me

I would try to convince people to agree with my thoughts.
I wanted them to purchase the same items that I bought.
I wanted people to practice the things I believed.
I wanted others to appreciate the insight I received.

I was controlling before I realized
that my life was being customized.
Soul searching became a game of hide and seek,
because I didn't see how my differences made me unique.

But today I am free because now I know,
that my high is my high and my low is my low.
My dreams are about who I want to be.
And I imagine the things that I want to see.

I understand that a song in which I find inspiration,
can cause another to change the radio station.
We all don't enjoy eating the same type of food.
We even express differently the same kind of mood.

The clothes we wear and what we watch on TV
are more elements of our individuality.
Attempts to change people was bad for my health,
because I lacked courage to be myself.

I used to find my preferences frustrating and confusing.
But I appreciate them now, and I find them amusing.
I cannot force things on people, I can only share.
If they are open and if they care.

Embracing differences in others has set me free.
So I no longer try to convince people to live like me.

Light Night

When times are so hard and rough,
some people give up on the positive stuff.
Deciding that enough is enough
and that embracing the darkness
means that they're tough.

And a part of them thinks that our optimism is strange,
because they don't believe that the bad things can change.
When they are immersed in a fear and a hate,
they see our trust and love and can't relate.

But they too can be gifted with this special sight
that allows them to see this light.
Because even though we keep our shine together,
we still can see the trouble.
And although we have our hope and faith,
we still can relate to the struggle.

We still keep a lot of people around
knowing that they could let us down.
It's all good,
because respected enemies are our friends,
because they are a helpful means to an end.

Even when things are out of place,
we manage to keep a smile on our face.
Although the night may seem cold and scary,
we know it's for a purpose that's temporary.

The Place to Be

Welcome…to this world. This is a private space.
This is an exclusive place.
There are so many loving others here
that there is nothing for you to fear.

When you step into this light, everything is al right
and there is not a problem in sight,
only solutions that we haven't implemented yet.
In this world, there are no regrets.

Only situations that we haven't learned from yet.
Over here we make no spiritual judgments.
We just see others that we don't understand yet.
So just take your shoes off.
And shake your blues off.

Simply come in and relax,
because you are no longer under attack.
Over here, you don't have to watch your back.
There is no need to.
Because the only person that can emotionally hurt you,
is you.

So just guard your own heart,
although we won't try to take it.
Hold it close because only you can break it.
By handing it over to someone else
and never learning to love God and yourself.

The Place to Be cont'd

In this world, love is your only invitation,
and you don't have to make any reservations.
Come here anytime while loving you,
so you can understand what and why we do.

Appreciating the constructive words that we say,
and why we choose to live our lives this way.
This is an experience you can't afford to miss,
because you have to see that this place exists.

This paradise is real.
And all that you have to do is heal,
and conquer your fears so you can start to feel.
Feel them, feel you, and even feel me,
because this is the place to be.

Do you know
that there is joy and peace right here on this earth?
For renewing your mind is the greatest rebirth.
Do you know,
that you don't have to wait until the next life
to be free from your fears, hatred and strife?

You can enjoy your life right here and right now.
And if you don't know how,
just ask yourself why can't you relate.
Start soul searching with no need to hesitate.

Beginning with only a thought in your mind,
about this place that is possible to find.
This world is not a fantasy. It is a reality.
Just renew your mind and elevate your mentality.

It is simply a matter of making a decision,
though this is not a club, cult or religion.
This is God's world, and it is up to you to see,
that this is really the place to be.

The Sky is Not the Limit!

The sky is high this we know.
Still there are no limits to where we can go.
So even if your goal seems so far away,
you are closer to reaching it day after day.

And as you go higher, things might seem strange,
because the atmosphere was designed to change.
But with a positive mentality you'll get things done,
and you'll conquer your fears just for fun.

Part Two:
Enlightened Love

Enlightened Love by Alicea Davis

This painting represents a person moving out of the
darkness of fear, into the light of trust.

A Queen's Dilemma

I am a woman who knows my worth.
I was destined for greatness since the day of my birth.
So I can't let my emotions get in the way,
of the role that I am supposed to play.

When I give my heart to a man,
he must understand just who I am.
There is a path that I must take.
If I don't, there is so much more at stake.

If I let my heart make my decision
it would change my chosen vision.
See, you make me feel like a woman,
but not like a queen.
And I don't want to live life in between.

Yes, you are a good man, but there's just this one thing.
I am supposed to wait for my king.
Still deep inside I have a fear
that I might regret it, if I don't stay right here.

And leaving isn't easy,
because I know you desire to please me.
I see you're trying so hard,
not to let down your guard.

A Queen's Dilemma cont'd

Even you try to protect your heart,
as you realize we are worlds apart.
I see that you are doing the best that you can.
I've even played with the thought of you being my man.

My emotions are telling me not to leave you alone.
But my mind is telling me to get back on my throne.
Because you make me feel like a woman
but not like a queen.
And I don't want to live life in between.

Yes, you are a good man, but there's just this one thing.
I am supposed to wait for my king.
Still deep inside I have a fear,
that I might regret it if I don't stay right here.

When a woman has so much strength inside,
it is only a king that won't let her hide.
Ordinary men think I'm dominant competition,
though a ruler will allow me my royal position.

The love is there, our feelings are strong,
but this is not the place that I belong.
It really breaks my heart to turn you down.
But I must wait for the man who wears the crown.

Because you make me feel like a woman
but not like a queen.
And I don't want to live life in between.
Yes, you are a good man, but there's just this one thing.
I am supposed to wait for my king.

The answer to my dilemma is to conquer the fear,
because I know I'll regret it if I stay right here.

May I Love You?

May I love you?
I mean the way that I want to?
Because I want to love you without any fear,
as if I have never cried a tear.

I want to say things to you that most are afraid to say,
because expressing my love will make my day.
Today, I am not scared,
I am fully prepared.

I want to give to you
just because…I want to.
And that is reason enough when the love is true.
Especially when I love you.

Baby when I love you, I'll love you
from wherever you are.
Just ask, how close is a shining star?
Answer is, it's close enough.
Close enough to shine on us when times get rough.

So no matter where in this world you might be,
you will always see love coming from me.
Because I can twinkle like a star in your darkest night,
or shine like the sun even when it's light.
But I want to know if that's all right.

And I know that it seems like I'm asking,
but I'm loving you already, and it's everlasting.
So you don't have to answer
because this love has begun.
I'm only asking right now just for fun.

May I love you?
Because this thing is more than make believe,
and I trust that you have the courage to receive.
I can't help but love you because I'm trusting me,
and I know this is how things are supposed to be.

I'm telling you that this is how I live,
and I won't be myself if I'm afraid to give.
So do you want me to or not?
Should I give you all that I've got?

With no hesitation...
with no unrealistic expectations...
and more importantly, with no expiration?

So not only can I love you,
I already do.
Though I can't help but ask...
may I love you?

Not to Love

See, that's why I decided not to love you
and to leave your memory behind.
Because it's torture just to have you dwelling in my mind.
So I know that if I let you in my heart,
my world would only break apart.

Things get broken when they are not handled properly.
That's what you did with my heart, my sacred property.
So why give my love to someone who doesn't care.
Why take my heart through unnecessary repairs?

If it's not broken, then don't break it.
If my heart is not yours, then don't try to take it.
You know I care about you; I won't try to fake it.
But deep down I know that we won't make it,
even if we make up.
I know we'll eventually forever break up.

Because I realize through our much needed space,
that my heart must reside in a safer place.
At least I have learned my lesson this time.
I'll share my love, but my heart is mine.

And that's why I decided not to love you.
I'm working hard to leave all those smiles behind.
Because it is torture to have you dwelling in my mind.
So, I know that if I let you in my heart,
that my world would only break apart.

I have sense enough to know,
that this has gone as far as it should go.
Because when I take a look at where we are,
I realize that we haven't gone very far.

And it's a shame because
we would have been really good friends
if I did not let other feelings come in.
Those feeling that were so deceiving,
that I prematurely starting believing,
that it was your love I would be receiving.

Luckily for my heart and me,
I'm secure enough to set you free.
So even though I care, I won't attempt to reach you.
I've learned from my mistakes,
but I won't attempt to teach you.

So if you don't believe that your partner is me,
then I'll have to move on and just let it be.
That's why I decided not to love you.
I'm leaving all those good times behind.
Because it's torture just to have you in mind.

It's so obvious that if I let you in my heart,
that my world would only break apart.
That's why I decided not to love you.
But the irony is, I already do.

Why else would I be writing this poem about you?

Bad Mouth

Ladies I just don't understand.
Why do you pick up the phone to call your friends,
just to bad mouth your man?
Don't you still need him?
Won't you still spoil and feed him?

Do you think your friends actually believe,
that you are tired enough to leave.
You two are staying together, and that's why you complain.
And this back and forth is only driving you insane.

Why gossip on the phone,
when you are not ready to leave him alone?
Because even though your stories are sad,
it is yourselves that you make look bad.

Because you might have reasons to walk away.
After you cry, you choose to stay.
And that's okay.
But the main reason why your friends may lend an ear,
is because your drama is so entertaining to hear.

You'll soon forget about all of that emotional harm.
By the end of the week, you'll be back in his arms.
So I really don't understand,
why would you bad mouth your man?

Since you are not ready to give him the boot,
it is best to keep your problems on mute.
Your friends don't need to be updated,
because when your man comes around them,
he'll sense that he's hated.

He'll wonder how could those words leave your mouth,
when your communication with him is headed south.
So no matter how much your friends may want to pry,
and wonder if he makes you cry,
just make the best of it.
And quietly work through the rest of it.

I am one who strongly believes,
that there is no use of complaining,
if you aren't willing to leave.
So do your relationship a favor.
Don't entertain them
by bad mouthing him.

Meant to Be

I am not feeling this potential relationship.
I am really not feeling this.
In the beginning should be an ignorant bliss.
Yet our infatuation phase was a hit and miss.

You being a decent man doesn't make you mine.
And I refuse to waste my precious time.
Today, days are weeks and weeks are years.
So why should I force myself to stay right here?

This thing is not meant to be,
when it is draining all of my energy.
I want to build up, and you want to tear down.
And I will not search through love's lost and found.

Although the time we spent was short and brief.
I can already see that you will cause me some grief.
I became familiar with your kind,
when I fast forwarded to our future, then pressed rewind,
because what I saw made me say, "Never mind."

The timing may not be right for you.
But it could be perfect for somebody new.
Right now a worthy prospect is starting to pray.
Let's listen in close to what he has to say.

"Lord let her be strong. Let her be wise.
Let me see Your light when I look into her eyes.
Let her be virtuous, strong and fine.
I promise to be a better man this time.
And, my lady, if you can hear me,
whether you are near or far,
I will be brought to wherever you are."

So I cannot stay here in the wrong person's face.
I need to clean out my personal space.
I am not about to give you my precious heart,
nor become the horse that pulls your cart.

You want to use the future as a dangling bait
and hope that I am foolish enough to wait.
But this opportunity is not for me.
Because it doesn't take wasted years for me to see,
that we were just not meant to be.

Love Digger

Fellas,
I know two types of women that are phony.
Using men for one reason only.
Tell me, is the woman who is financially greedy,
worse than the woman who is emotionally needy?
I think not.
Even though both have a plot
to take you for all that you've got.

One wants to leave you with only a dime,
while the other wants to take up all of your time,
and both are a crime.
But the woman who is emotionally needy,
is the one who is extremely greedy.

That man she is with, she could care less about him.
She was attached like this to the rest of them.
You see, with a love digger, it is never about the man.
He is just another victim of her plans.

She doesn't have standards. He could be wealthy.
He could be a bum.
He could be as low as scum.
Because all of that doesn't matter,
when it's love that she's after.

Desperate for love, she digs through your soil,
not knowing that she will never strike oil.
Because no matter how much you show her that you care,
she's afraid that one day, you won't be there.

Meanwhile, she's on the prowl,
to somehow,
find love right now.
So, fellas, be on high alert,
of these love diggers so full of pain and hurt,
that all you have to is flirt
before you can take off her skirt.

The love digger means no disrespect.
It's just because of so much neglect,
that things have become complex.
This woman thinks that love is sex.
You must resist the temporary pleasure of sin at night,
causing her to never let you leave her sight.
No dollar signs are in her eyes,
just lonely hearts pierced with darts.
She didn't overcome all of her hurt and pain,
so she searches for a man to exhaust and drain.
You think she is a psycho chick,
but she is a love digger who is emotionally sick.

And about that brick that she used to bust up your truck,
it wasn't because you ran out of luck.
That episode wasn't even about you.
But about all of those other men that she dug through.

Are you wondering why she keeps blowing up your phone,
even though you want her to leave you alone?
Well, this love digger has a high tolerance for hurt.
She won't leave just because you treat her like dirt.

Fellas, it's easier to be cold,
to the woman that is digging for gold.
You see, with a gold digger, you can just cut off her funds,
if you want to send her on the run.
But those love diggers are hard to drop
without you having to call the cops.

Love Digger cont'd

She can't fathom the thought of losing you,
because that would mean that those lies
from her childhood were true.
But the truth is, you two might have worked out,
if she wasn't full of so much insecurity and doubt.

Now she's back to crying on Kleenex tissues,
because she hasn't pulled out those deep rooted issues.
That's why she will have feelings so strong,
for the very next man that comes along.

Fellas, you better watch out; she is coming your way.
That woman that will listen to every word you say.
You think it's because your game is tight,
Or you are worth a meaningless catty fight.

Sorry buddy, but it's a fact
that her motives are not even set on that.
You are not running game,
when her past is the blame.

You're just putting yourself in danger,
playing with a love digger that is full of anger.
So trust me, let the truth be told;
she is worse than the woman who is digging for gold.

You must prepare for the woman who already knows
that she has love,
because she is the daughter of our God above.

I'm Learning Him

I'm learning him from the inside out.
I want to know without a doubt,
what this man is all about.
Now, even though I have a schoolgirl crush,
this is a process that cannot be rushed.
Because if I'm impatient,
his intentions would be hushed.

I'm only open to that man
who'll give me the love that I deserve.
So even though I'm feeling him,
I'll just sit back and observe.
I want to know how he carries his wit and his charm,
and if he's holding someone in his masculine arms.

I wish to learn about his aspirations and plans,
and how he works with his mind and talented hands.
Then when I find out what he intends to do,
I'll wonder if he is the type that will follow through.
Is he my true companion indeed?
Does he have that mindset to protect and feed?

Is he the type to hold an ambitious woman back?
Or does he admire a woman
who can make her money stack?
Does he have the desire to control me?
Or does he respect me as a person equally?

I'm Learning Him cont'd

What is his idea of strength and security?
Can I enjoy his spiritual maturity?
And even if my questions are based out of fear.
I'll use them to my advantage before I let him near.
These are things that I want to see.
They are qualities that are important to me.

I know that I am not asking for much,
when it comes down to the person that my soul will touch.
Before I attract what I want,
my essence must be the same.
Otherwise my energy and character will be the blame.

If he's for me, I'll know by the smiles on my face,
and how my world will continue to be a warm place.
We'll have the freedom to push our inhibitions away.
While he's learning me as well, and I'm making his day.
I trust that he is selective too,
for we must be careful in what we do.

We're learning each other not too fast or too slow.
Because we both have places that we want to go.
And no matter how much of him I am privileged to explore,
I know I can always learn about him some more.
Our lesson plan is coming along so far so good.
I know our connection is understood.

And only time will tell me if I'm hanging out on a limb,
because today I'm taking a risk, and I'm learning him.

Beauty

I don't know who other women may want to be,
but my standard of beauty happens to be me.
I'm not comparing myself to those chicks on TV.
What's the point, when I can look at me?

I look within to see that beauty is mine.
So how dare society attempt to define.
With darker? Lighter?
Wronger? Righter?
This or that?
Thin? Fat?

Sheer perfection? Or a genetic mistake?
Please, give me a break!
I wish that the women would stop
competing and comparing.
And realize that the men will never stop staring.

They will always stare at her, me and you.
So just be yourself and do what you want to do.
There is only one person that I want to be,
because my standard of beauty will always be me.

Emotions

Are our emotions illusions
that we perceive to be real?
Are we conditioned to create,
the way that we feel?

Relationships

Relationships are to be enjoyed,
not taken for granted or destroyed.
Because people do not have to be near us.
They could distance themselves, if they dislike or fear us.

It is a compliment to your energy and essence,
if a person chooses to be in your presence.
So handle them with care and treat them good.
Let your appreciation for them be understood.

Whether they are familiar to you
or if they are a stranger,
their well-being should not be in danger.
For to hurt others is to hurt yourself.
Respecting people is good for your spiritual health.

The world does not have to be lonely or cold,
when there are people around with hands to hold.
There is a warm and loving place to be found,
when you value the people who are near and around.

This poem is dedicated to my entire family.
Hi Layna!

I Can Feel

I was hurt as a child and even as an adult.
So a cold-hearted woman was the result.
I couldn't accept pleasure for trying to block out the pain.
My sense of compassion was going down the drain.

So when a good man would approach me and try to come
close,
I would treat him as if he were a ghost.
His presence was hazy because my mind was unclear.
His sweet words were sounds that my heart wouldn't hear.

His qualities I didn't appreciate or receive,
because to me, they were only make-believe.
Then one day, after I let some good ones slip away,
I lifted my head to say, "I cannot live my life this way!"

And this new light that I was seeing,
made me a more constructive being.
So I took my heart and I did the unthinkable.
I wanted to test if love was truly unsinkable.

I thawed my heart that was cold and numb,
and warmed it up for a special someone.
It actually felt good.
And this trust thing was being more understood.

The warm tears from my eyes were a blessing so real.
They were evidence that once again,
I can feel.

This poem is dedicated to my husband, Benjamin Davis.

Part Three:
Barriers Broken

Barriers Broken by Alicea Davis

This painting symbolizes people appreciating differences in others.

Grateful

This message is for all of the whites
who've always had the desire to love and unite.
You were the ones who had our backs
and did not prejudge us because we were black.

You are more than an exception
to all that hatred and rejection.
You were our trusted ally,
when we needed help to get by.

You were against all the suffering that we went through.
Although we were the victims, you cried too.
And we are so grateful
for you not being hateful.

In a time where discrimination is still tried and true,
we have to give credit to whom honor is due.
Today, when I needed a job to pay my bills,
you didn't focus on my color, but you admired my skills.

Yesterday, when we marched, I know you took pride.
As we protested for civil rights, you were right by our side.
And the day before, when the slaves hid underground,
my family took shelter in your home,
though you pretended that they were not around.

And we are so grateful
for you not being hateful.
Especially in those times
when loving us was a crime.

Grateful cont'd

You risked your own kindred's respect and trust,
all in the name of helping us.
As we celebrated Emancipation,
you were dancing and drinking,
instead of questioning, "What was Lincoln thinking?"

It is amazing through all the pain and insanity,
how you managed to keep your love and humanity.
You let your children play with us.
You came to church to pray with us.

It is nice to see you more than once in a while,
when you genuinely greet us, with your welcoming smile.
Even though there is still room to grow,
we appreciate you, and we want you to know,

we still need you
Because uniting humanity is what we can do.
I see you, my friend.
Making it easier as our struggle
comes close to an end.

The truth is,
there are still some inequalities out there.
But we know better than to think that you do not care.
And we are just so grateful
for you not being hateful.

Thank you.

Unite and Conquer (evolved)

A nation that is divided will fall.
So we all must come together to build up a wall.
As long as there is hatred between white and black,
we're all vulnerable to this country being attacked.
White and black...black and white.
Will we finally get this thing right?

Notice that what I am saying may pertain to you,
whether you look brown, yellow, red or blue.
Although there is more to us, than a shade or color,
this racial epidemic affects the way we view one another.
Day after day, I am more convinced,
that racism is only a symptom, of what we're up against.

We are challenging the spirit of fear,
and only love can make it disappear.
Oh yes, fear was the engrained seed
that brought forth hatred, discrimination and greed.
And now more love is all that we need.
It's in the best interest of this land being free,
that we must invest in a greater bond between you and me.

Will the division come to an end,
if we challenge where this outlook began?
Achieving unity requires trust and bravery,
to question if we're all negatively affected
by war and slavery.

Unite and Conquer (evolved) cont'd

I'm just searching for the light to leave hatred behind.
I know that changing laws will not change the heart
and the mind.
Has the past made you fearful too?
Are hurtful views embedded inside of you?
Do you trust that the stereotypes are true?
Or is your heart yearning for something new?

The fear of differences, our hearts must fight it,
so all the citizens in this land can be united.
The fact that this country is now diverse,
must be accepted and not be reversed.
We are all connected. We are all affected.
And everyone must be respected.

We have dominion over the earth's food chain.
So why cause a fellow human being hurt and pain?
When you explore the galaxies in outer space,
you'll find that we must survive in this place.
So why judge another because of their race,
if you love the image that is on your face?

It is unity that will keep this country strong.
So we all must feel that we belong.
This is not a one-sided quest for unity.
We must build up the mindsets in every community.
Challenging us all to face and conquer our past.
Or is that too much for me to ask?

Freedom's Burden

Freedom? You want to know about freedom?
Well, being free
is not as easy as I thought it would be.
In fact, being free has become a burden
that is so full of pain,
because now I see the people wearing invisible chains.

And these mental chains are not an illusion.
Yet I refuse to accept a negative conclusion.
I am traveling this journey that is freeing my mind,
and I don't want to leave the people behind.

I was in mental bondage,
and it was hard breaking through.
So, I understand why freedom
may be intimidating to you.

But delivering others from mental oppression
has become my obsession.
Getting people to think and move
in a more positive direction.

Because I know that our problems will not always last.
I see a bright future coming from our dark past.
But it's a burden to be free,
because it's my responsibility
to help the people to see who they can potentially be.
I can't enjoy this freedom selfishly.

Freedom's Burden cont'd

The need for mental freedom is often misunderstood.
That's why outsiders focus on the surface
of broken neighborhoods.
Certain charities and some celebrities
want to lend a helping hand.
But at times it seems, that most don't understand,
why many urban communities are poor on this land.

Their heartfelt donations may not produce lasting fruit,
if we don't pluck the ghetto's problems up from their roots.
So boarding up abandoned houses and
building playgrounds is not all it's about,
when the ghetto needs a makeover
from the inside out.

Don't get me wrong. Good intentions are fine.
But efforts may be in vain,
if we are not freeing urban minds.
If we don't put this mental struggle to an end,
the cleaned up ghettos might get messed up again.

It's not just the time for that bucket of paint and soap.
If you want to make a difference,
also give these children some hope.

Say to them, "Young man, no matter your mistakes,
you come from greatness and that makes you great."
Tell that young sister, "Your natural beauty is fine,
but give your soul permission to shine."

We must educate our youth on our economic power,
and how we can upgrade our own community,
with our own dollars.
Let them know that they can achieve material success,
and still be mentally oppressed.
Besides, "what is the purpose behind building wealth,
if you've never had the luxury of being yourself?"

Because our people are unique!
And when we smother that truth,
it lowers the self-esteem of our developing youth.
They appear to express rebellion rather than pride,
when society suppresses who they are inside.

It seems that our youth are confused
about who they are supposed to be.
As a people, are we even culturally free?
Or is oppression still festering in our community?
Are we influenced to endure an identity removal,
that may train us to seek society's approval?

Are these insecurities misunderstood,
when the focus is on the surface
of low income neighborhoods?
If we are still defining who we are,
after that's established we can really go far.

Freedom's Burden cont'd

So I use my voice as a contribution,
hoping that together we will implement
the greatest solution.
Although this outlook is obvious for me to see,
people have to decide who they want to be.

And if what I'm saying makes sense to you,
then imagine all the building that we could do.
Although people have been
spreading this message for years,
hopefully this time around it is loud and clear.

The ignorance was bliss,
but now I have knowledge that I can't dismiss.
This freedom is a burden that I bear,
and if more people will take their fair share,
it would be a better world out there.

February

People why do we think that it's scary,
to talk about our history when it's not February.
Like all of a sudden we become aware,
of a history that is always there.
In February we remember about that dream
from the honorable Dr. King.
And in February, it's
Lift every voice and sing
Till' earth and heaven ring.
But by March the 1st, I think it's a shame,
how our lives and our progress may still be the same.
Has our culture been reduced to a holiday and a game?
Our story has the power to build up other races,
once we rise up from stereotypical places,
and start appreciating the beauty
of our own minds and faces.
And somebody please tell me why…
Why do we only light firecrackers on the 4th of July?
When 1776 was not our year of independence.
That year we were not free.
We were still in slavery.
So while we're standing over that barbecue grill
and putting ribs in our mouths, let's just keep it real.
While they were talking about
how the stars were spangled,
our people were in captivity still being strangled.
So let's honor January 1st of 1865.
The day Emancipation helped our people to survive.
Because the only thing to me that seems to be scary,
is that we're proud to be ourselves in February.

Black On Purpose (evolved)

I used to question what my life was about.
But now without a shadow of a doubt,
I know so many reasons why I am here.
And why I don't have to live my life in fear.

I'm talking about reasons that caused me
to break out of confinement,
to get busy on my divine assignment.
But first, I had to search beneath the surface
to see that God created me black on purpose.

This is all about me being black,
because my cultural esteem was once under attack.
They say that the label black may be culturally outdated.
Because it's connected to a past where our colors were
separated.
I'll still use it to get my point across,
so that our sense of identity will not be lost.

I understand that our character
is not determined by the color of our skin.
I know that we are all connected
by the light that shines within.
But I am still black – on purpose.

And as much as I appreciate everyone else,
I have to take this moment to celebrate myself.
Because I could have been born into any other race.
I could be wearing an entirely different face.
But I'm black!

There are no coincidences when it comes down to me.
Even the year I was born was a part of my destiny.

Because of my strong optimistic ways
I am a part of these changing days.
This is the era in which I am placed,
and my contributions cannot be erased.
Because I am here on purpose.

And I can't hide myself any longer,
when my struggles have made me stronger.
The more I see, the more I realize,
that my hair and my skin are a symbol and a prize.

I remind the world of a battle that humanity won.
And how we were victorious over slavery
centuries before it begun.
Because God allowed that on purpose too.

American slavery taught the world that,
chains can be forced on your body and mind,
and freedom may seem impossible to find.
But when you trust in the Lord
and work towards a better day,
you can make your struggles go away!

I know that God made me black on purpose.
And this thing goes way beneath the surface.
God made you on purpose too.
So let's unleash our greatness
and see what we can do.
I know that God made me black on purpose.

Love Locs

To dread means to have great fear.
But I am the opposite of the negativity that you hear.
So, who dreads the locs on my head? Not me.
I have nothing but love for my locs, you see.

I do not dread the pattern of unity
that my hair naturally follows when I just let it be.
That's why I have never called them dreadlocks.
They are lovelocs to me.
I do not dread the strength and beauty I see.

My lovelocs do not represent my rebellion towards man,
but an acceptance of God's divine creativity and plan.
Single strands of my hair are now locked together
throughout my head,
and I refuse to adopt the concept of dread.

I used to straighten my hair with chemicals or with a
burning hot press.
But now my hair has gone through
its natural locking process.
My new mindset requires my locs to have a positive name,
because I wear them with love and not with shame.

Love is a feeling of deep affection.
So I wear my lovelocs without dreading others' rejection.
I only focus on the acceptance that I have from above,
while wearing my locs with care and love.

Women Like Me

I am sick and tired of this mess,
waiting for reparations that still need to be addressed!
This is not about 40 acres and a mule.
I'm not holding my breath; I'm not a fool.
I know that this world can be cruel.

This is about the men in our own community
who have not given back,
to the women who've endured
while their minds are off track.

Women who've stood by our men
since that shipment arrival.
Women who've dedicated their lives
to our people's survival.

And I take this reparations thing personally,
because I'm speaking up for women like me.
We were ripped from your arms, but we stayed.
They tried to break us down, but we prayed,
so we can still be a family. But you've strayed.
I have respect and appreciation for diversity.
But let's face the fears between you and me.

Today, not enough husbands and fathers
are in our homes.
Women are having to make it on their own.
It's like our future together is almost gone.

Women Like Me cont'd

Yet, I have faith that somewhere out there
that there are more men in this community
who know and care.
After our grandparents tore down the walls of segregation,
our people scattered in a massive separation.
Though gaining the freedom of integration
was necessary for our progress,
we seemed to have lost our sense of unity
throughout the process.

As we strive to get our community under control,
we need to take pride in our privileged roles.
When love and trust was nowhere around.
the family unit is where strength and motivation
was found.

That's why I take this reparations thing personally,
because I'm speaking up for women like me.
I'm not speaking up for those
who are full of bitterness and resentment,
but for us women
who are sticking by our historic commitment.
Women like me.

And I'm not speaking up for those
who don't understand
the challenges that we've conquered
while here on this land,

but for us women who build with a loving hand.
Women like me.

I'm not speaking up for those women
who buy that nice house and car,
then all of a sudden forget how valuable you are.
But for us women who remember that you are a star.
Women like me.

I'm proudly representing the women
from our story's beginning,
who weren't this close to our happy ending,
who passed on this message
that right now I am sending.

"Women hold on. Men come home.
Women hold on. Men come home."

Please understand that life is not only about you.
Take a look at the timeline,
and what we are going through.
We need you now more than ever without a doubt,
because our community is facing a potential burnout.

So we apologize if we come across rude.
We apologize if we offend you with our attitude.
We will even control our snappy temper.
Though it's not easy working with heroes
who don't seem to remember.

Women Like Me cont'd

Remember that we have a greater job to do.
Remember that we are somebody's ancestors too.
Remember to appreciate the women
who are connected to you,
because together our community will make it through.

I trust that this historic compensation
is not just a figment of my imagination.
I view this relative situation
and only yearn for more participation.

As I look back at our efforts, it breaks my heart,
to think that our people will forever be torn apart.
And I'm taking this reparations thing personally,
because I'm speaking up for women like me.

Triumphant Woman

Day by day I'm learning the magnitude,
of me being a triumphant woman
with a positive attitude.

Possessing the power and passion that promotes unity,
with love to give to the world and to my community.
Because I was blessed enough to identify and dismiss,
subliminal problems that some don't realize exist.
And if what I've said so far isn't making any sense,
just let me inform you on what I was up against.

You see, I was taught to care,
if other people look and stare.
I was conditioned to be insecure
about revealing my African hair.
But I have learned to love my precious coils,
so, no more harsh chemicals, only natural oils.

And society told me,
that I might become another Negro whore.
Yet I am privileged to know I am so much more.
This woman isn't just for the bedroom
but also the living room, the dining room
and even out of the front door.
Because I am made with ambition! I am made to soar!

Triumphant Woman cont'd

And society told me,
"Your father doesn't care about you."
But they'd failed to tell me that he'd be triumphant too!
After all these years, I am blessed to see
we will always be a family.
I am a part of a dynamic legacy.

And society told me to just give up on our men.
Since the majority are either unemployed
or locked up in the pen.
But they didn't tell me
that our men are too strong for defeat.
And they didn't tell me
that our men would land on their feet.

It is their triumph that I admire and respect.
It is triumph that I am honored to project.
And back in slavery,
the mothers taught that the way to survive
was to obey the master to stay alive.

But it's a new day, and I will teach them the truth.
Building up their self-esteem in the days of their youth.
I'll teach them not to be mentally deaf or blind.
I'll show them our future
so that they won't be left behind.

Directing them to where our people
are yearning to be.
And when they are ready to lead,
they will start to teach me.

As our people continue to get back together,
we will inspire other communities to be even better.
The world needs our people and so do I.
Let's stick together and reach beyond the sky.
I'll make a difference because I know the magnitude,
of being a triumphant woman
with a positive attitude.

About the Author

God is healing and empowering the minds of others through the uplifting poetry and insightful artwork of Alicea Davis. She has been writing poetry for over 25 years which began in her childhood. She is passionate about creating work that will be a resource of light in our world.

Born and raised in Detroit, MI, Alicea launches projects that the whole world can experience. Her first book entitled *The Sky is NOT the Limit: A Book of Empowering Poetry* inspires readers to transition from the darkness of fear into the light of trust in multiple areas of life. *From Hatred to Healing: Eight Racial Reconciliation Poems* offers much hope, as it takes readers on a journey of healing from deep mistrust due to racial injustice. It inspires racial reconciliation in order to change the painful history of racism in America.

Davis is also a talented visual artist. Her paintings communicate deep truths and emotions that words alone cannot convey. Davis has shared her messages with the masses on television, radio, at universities and more. Visit her website www.AliceaDavis.com to learn more about her and her work.

CPSIA information can be obtained
at www.ICGtesting.com
Printed in the USA
FFHW022247231118
49518024-53878FF